Storm Biscuits

Also By Pauline Prior-Pitt

WAITING WOMEN (1989)
(Revised edition in 1999 after 7 reprints)
ISBN 1 872916 29 5

ADDRESSES & DREAMS (1997)
(Revised edition 2004)
ISBN 1 872916 28 7

IRONING WITH SUE LAWLEY (2005)
ISBN 1872916 34 1

Poetry Pamphlets
These are handmade handstitched pamphlets 15 cm square

NORTH UIST SEA POEMS (2005)
ISBN 1872916 36 8
Winner of the 2006 Callum Macdonald Award for Pamphlet Poetry

THREE SCORE YEARS & SOME (2005)
ISBN 1872916 37 6

Front Cover illustration by Robert Prior-Pitt

PAULINE PRIOR-PITT

STORM BISCUITS

SPIKE PRESS

Storm Biscuits
First published in 2001 by SPIKE PRESS

Reprinted: 2003, 2007

Publisher: SPIKE PRESS
112 Broomfield Road, Coventry, CV5 6JZ.
Tel: 01876 560360

Distributor: AVANTI BOOKS
Unit 9, The io Centre, Whittle Way, Arlington Business Park,
Stevenage, SG1 2BD. Tel: 01438 747000

Printed and Bound in Scotland by Nevisprint Ltd,
Unit 3, Caol Industrial Estate, Fort William, PH33 7PH

ISBN 1 8729 31 7

For more details about poems, performances,
after dinner speaking, and book orders,
visit:
www.pauline-prior-pitt.com

Pauline Prior-Pitt is a freelance writer, performer and after dinner speaker. She now lives with her husband on the Isle of North Uist in the Outer Hebrides but still travels to the mainland several times a year to give performances and to see her three children and her grandsons.

ACKNOWLEDGEMENTS

Several of these poems first appeared in THE MAGAZINE and in AN T-UIBHISTEACH

Four poems, Summer Light, Winter Light, Down the Machair Path, and No Escape, first appeared under the title **Exposed Island**, which was commissioned by the Warwick Festival for its weekend of contemporary music in July 2002. The music was composed by Karen Wimhurst for speaking voice, flutes and guitar and was performed by Pauline Prior-Pitt, the Scottish Flute Trio and Alan Neeve.

for Robert

CONTENTS

TELEPHONE CALL

Of course there's running water
yes, cold and hot.
And electricity.
And heating. Not

main drainage no,
but we've a septic tank
and to be frank
we've had no trouble.

Lonely, only if you want to be.

Not far from the sea.

Stunning; deserted beaches
silver shell sand
turquoise indigo seas
distant purple headlands.

Oh very friendly
very friendly indeed.

There's a Co-op nearby
you can get everything you need.

Well fresh pasta, fajitas, fruit, veg,
live yoghurt, the usual supermarket food.

Lorries arrive three times a week.
The quality of everything is very good.

Yes it is quiet,
so quiet you can hear the beat of a seagull's wing.

No I can't say that I really miss anything.

Absolutely pitch black at night.
The stars are so bright.

Mm, yes, sometimes,
in the winter, Northern Lights.

Single track with passing places
everyone waves. No one races along
well that's not quite true
some people do.

Gales? Oh very strong,
stronger than anything I've ever known
but I've grown used to them.
Don't like to go out on my own
in case I get blown away.

It's never too hot,
but in July and August,
brave swimmers swim a lot
I do on sunny days
when the tide comes in
across warm sand bays

Plenty of places, hills, moors,
beaches for walking
and there's canoeing and fishing
if that's what you're wanting

Wellingtons, walking boots,
scarf, hat, waterproof gear
and shorts and bathing things.
In one day we can have all the seasons of the year.

Yes you must
Do come
I'm sure you'll love it here .

DOWN THE MACHAIR PATH

Down the machair path
in mist so low
it touches the scrub willow

starlings arrange themselves
on a stave of wires
like the opening notes
of an accidental concerto

through the mist
a sudden flat disc sun
conjures a white rainbow
across the fallow

and ragged cattle
caught in the spotlight
don't know they're sitting
on a crock of gold.

Machair is a gaelic word for the rich fertile land
which lies behind the dunes. It is covered in shell sand
which blows over during winter storms.

ROCK

Wherever you look,
rock is poking through
leaving the grass behind.

Huge boulders,
on the point of balance
look as if they are about to fall

and stones
that stand still
form an ancient circle.

Loose rocks litter the hillside
and rocks, that once were houses,
byres and field walls lie in heaps.

You notice shelter stones
whose leeward sides
sprout pale green lichen spikes

and where the sea
has heaped up shingle, there are
spaces between steep rocks

where flat stones,
warmed by the sun,
make perfect hiding places.

DESERTED CROFT HOUSE

From the road, it looks like a child's drawing,
a chimney at each end, door
in the middle, windows either side.

Mountains are in the distance
with a glimpse of sea. The sun
is a spikey yellow flower.

The door isn't locked, of course,
no one does and anyway
the windows are square holes.

If the dust wasn't so deep,
you could think she had just gone
down to the shore to gather driftwood.

Her small purse is open on the table
next to a cup and saucer
and a pinafore is set on the back of a chair

as if someone called her name
a moment ago and she took it off
to answer the door.

You love it, want to buy it, spend
the rest of your life restoring it,
replacing rotten timbers and roof tiles,

pointing up the stones, painting them white,
putting in heat and light. You know exactly
how it's going to look. But it's not for sale.

They say it used to be a ceilidh house
where every night the sounds of songs
and stories warmed these crumbling walls.

And somehow you know the house is waiting,
holding its breath, for when she walks back in
and sets the driftwood in the grate.

A MAKING MAN

How you saw rough wood
clamp the lengths together
fix wire and fine green net
across the spaces
making fences for our garden
protection against storms.

How often on the journey
have you made fences
in our landscape
created spaces out of fences
mended fences
worked with wood.

How your fences have been
for keeping some out
and letting others in
sheltered by your fences
made sure, made safe.

How later you will paint
a fine watercolour.
Frame it in smoothed pine.

EXPOSING THE ROCK

She took a sledgehammer
to the coal store
outside the back door.

Broke the ugly concrete-blocks
into hard core. Then slice by slice
removed soft turf. And digging deep

filled forty barrow loads with earth
and stones. She scraped
and scoured the last remaining soil

and brushed away fine dust
until the rock appeared.
A steady downpour washed it clean.

And there it is. Outcrop of gneiss,
solid cream grey swirling rock,
rust patched in places

laminated with rich quartz ,
striated in deep grooves
where ancient ice crushed past.

A hollow in the rock has filled with rain
to make a bath for sparrows. And in
sharp crevices white pebbles look like waterfalls.

STARLINGS

squadrons of starlings
line up on wires
ready for take off

on stone chimney pots
starlings warm their tails
singing like blackbirds

rain fills the hollow
sparrows sit and wait
starlings are bathing

in red post boxes
starlings build their nests
sheltered from the wind

black arrow jets in
perfect formation
starlings on the wing

NOT QUITE PREPARED

I have enjoyed each decade in my life
Though each has caught me out not quite prepared.
And now as I leave sixty years behind
And roll along towards my seventh round
It's time to look about and take some thought,
Plan how to spend the last remaining years
So when I reach the time when all things pause
I won't look back and feel dissatisfied.

I'll travel to the far side of the world
Bathe naked every day in foaming seas.
And see my children once a week at least.
Or maybe I shall still be unprepared,
I'll be with friends still chattering away
And death will catch me even as I speak.

MILES AWAY: A GRANDMOTHER IN WAITING

Gales are forecast in the Outer Hebrides.
Already white horses crest the waves.
The sea is bright green in one last spike
of sun against dark grey.

Above my desk, her photograph
with curls, blue eyes that
trust me, match the denim jacket
Dad bought for a surprise.

We giggle on the phone. Talk
about her light domestic duties,
think of silly names to call her baby
Mangle? Sausage? Fridge?

She says the baby's room is sea-side,
the floor painted blue for water, sand yellow
by the door. Mobile dolphins hang above
the basket cradle covered in white cotton.

Midwives have prepared her for the labour.
A birthing pool. It's calm in there, sheltered.
Miles away, inland, her baby
will be born into the water.

At the sea's edge, mighty wave-towers
crash, curl over, smash white onto rocks.
Angry water heaves up boulders.
Tasting salt, I call her name into the wind.

LATE ADVENTURE

Lean on the wind, swept
by giant's breath onto this island

gale force nine
increasing to storm force ten.

Stand where beaches curve
silver to the sea's deep turquoise.

Hold silence in shielded granite space
below clear horizons.

Lose control.
Catch up with Vikings.

Believe something is held here
waiting.

SEA

arriving at the sea

it is as if
until this moment
we have held our breath
tight in our chests
and only now
dare to let go

as if in towns
and cities
we are not free
and only the sea
releases us

secretly
we are all in love
with the sea.

SHORE

wind spin
sea drift
soft rain veils

wave lace
edges
blow apart

in bubbles
skimming
water

sand
curves
to pebble clusters

high tide
heaps
a charnel-house

bleached thighs
of dry
sea tangle

hold eye
spy grey seals
watching

DUNE

standing in
marram grass
high above

a half moon
bay of silver
shell sand

no trace
of footprints
sheltering down

shifting
sand-blow
uncovers flotsam

wet rope
drift wood
plastic orange floats

sand crack
sandslipping
down dissolving

in emerald water
toppling
over

and over
in high winter
storm tides

FULMARS

Fulmars glide
stiff winged
wave skim
kiss in pairs
on steep cliffs

NAMING : ØY, AY, ISLAND

hill island, Vallay
bear island, Bernaray
tidal island, Oronsay

seal island, Shillay
yellow, pleasant, Wiay
hermit island, priest, Pabbay

Channel of the Swan
on either side lie
Groatay and Hermetray

Grim's island, Grimsay
big raft island, Flodday
a prominent hill, Tahay

rough island, Ronay
fort island, Bororay
island with a bay, Vaccasay

long island on the sea's edge
Havbrødøy, Hebrides

RETRACING
(walking back from Udal)

Walking back along the shore
I see my early footsteps
still going out, taking me there

to the headland, tumble outcrop,
table of rock, an altar
for imagined sacrifice.

My footprints disappear
into heaped pebbles. I smooth
clusters in my pockets

sinking prints left
high and dry by the tide
go striding past in wavy lines

long detours branch off
into sand dunes, come
running back to the waterline.

I walk side by side
step into my tracks
match my stride

overlapping in circles
slow dancing
in and out of the sun.

Rooting back my time's
running out. I march
in a straight line

to where the stream flows
wide across the beach
deeper now on the incoming tide

I cross higher up
not my usual place
wading through fast water

onto mud at the other side,
leaving squelched prints.
Nothing much to go on.

When I reach the rocks
I have to cross, slippery sea-wrack
will cover my tracks.

SUMMER LIGHT

think of green water

no, turquoise
think of blue
more green than blue

no, more blue than green
but darker
ultramarine

no, deeper turquoise
emerald sapphire

think of them all

think of sand cream bays
when the tide is out
streaked with shallow pools
reflecting silver blue

no, make that milky green

though milky green is more when the
tide saunters back in
and water from the burn
mingles peat brown to violet streams.

think bright green

no, brighter
a may green, like leaf buds
of rowan trees in spring
machair headlands turning
daisy white to pansy yellow
buttercup to clover pink

think all this together

WINTER LIGHT

Think mostly muted
as if seen through grey veils

still think abundant green, duller
water-logged brown in places
moss green fringed fawn

think cinnamon and ginger
think peat brown dug deep, almost black
think grey burns, grey lochs
grey sea trailing white spray.

Then think a low down sun
think peat grass glowing crimson
on the hill

think marram glossing ochre
over pale sand against gold water

think brimming burns and lochs
holding ink blue light.

DUNE DINOSAURS

Out on the machair
dune dinosaurs rest
their rusted bones in hollows

you come across them
picking your way through clover
searching for orchids

this flattened binder
spread out like a diagram
of flaking parts

that collapsed tractor
stripped to the bone
in buttercups and daisies

did they seize up here
sink into some too soft earth
and refuse to move

or were they brought here
to their final resting place
left to rust as an

added attraction
for tourists: rare birds, wild flowers
and dune dinosaurs.

NO ESCAPE

You can't escape the wind here.
It penetrates your waking dreams
in endless symphony.

Rasps its bow on leafless twigs
of scrub willow that dare to jut
above the sheltering wall.

Scrapes to shrieking pitch
electric wires stretched
taut across the land.

Snatches quick grace notes
where seed heads quake,
seed heads quake in flattening grass.

And round the outside
corners of the house
it rolls a constant drum.

Once in a while, at sunset,
exhausted by its frantic day, it rests
and there is silence in the Western Isles.

STORM

The storm
cracks its whip
at the wind

wind so strong
it smacks eyes to tears
lashes cheeks into red rashes

buckles your knees
makes you run
not to fall over

wind so strong it howls
prowls in and out
of houses

roof tiles rattle
and windows catch
the snare and snatch of hail

black plastic
fraps to shreds
on barbed wire fences

wind so strong
the sea seethes white.

STORM BISCUITS
(circa 1950, for Peggie Hill)

A sudden rush of battering wind
slaps hail hard on our windows, waking us.
Above our heads, loose slates begin
their dancing on the roof. Drowsy in the dark

drifting in and out of sleep we dream
of nightmare waves towering our loch
drowning our croft like a sandcastle, leaving no trace
and we're wide awake, wanting to be safe.

Our mother fears to sleep and creeps downstairs
to set the peats and light the tilley lamp
above the stove. We hear her move about
the house and wrapped in blankets we go down.

She has already beaten sugar, butter, flour
Into a shortbread paste and with an upturned
glass is cutting circle shapes and in
the middle, with a thimble, cuts a hole.

She makes about two dozen, bakes them
in the oven by the fire. We roll the bits.
When they're done she sticks together
twos with jam and puts white icing on.

And now, in the middle of the night
she feeds us her storm biscuits, pours warm milk
into our mugs to help us sleep. Says
there will be no school for us tomorrow.

NO SIGNAL

Hanging on the phone,
music in my ear
I wouldn't choose. Yearning tracks
"You can say what you want,
say what you want about,
say what you want about me.

I feel the same about you."
A voice apologises for any inconvenience
my call will be answered as soon as....
and thanks me for my patience.
"about you I feel the same
you can say what you want"

Tracey speaking on behalf
of Vodaphone asks how she can help.
Can she help me. I tell her there's
no service on my mobile. She says
I'm living in a black hole.
There are no plans for a signal.

Black hole, where turquoise
overlapping aquamarine seas
surge to silver sand shores
where green dunes stipple cinnamon
against gentle cardboard cut out
hill on hill, misty, heather, gold.

Black hole, black night, black sea roar.
Crossing the black moor,
a single track with passing places.
No one passes my stopped car.
And I can't signal, can't say what I want
and I don't feel the same.

WATER

Surrounded by water,
sea lochs seek to invade
the land at high tide.

And inland, fresh water lochs
are scattered as if
flung from some giant hand.

Lochs set like jewels,
mirror blue skies
reflect back ultramarine

and even on a day of dullest grey
water echoes silver.

HOUSE FUNERAL

Norman MacDonald, who could
have played for Scotland
died on Sunday March 11th aged 58.

Norman, the unique man, leader
of the pack, struck down years ago
A young man in a wheel chair

His brother and sister close by his side.

So popular, he knew the score of more
than football matches. So witty, he could
always joke and make his nurses laugh.

Friends called in everyday, and everywhere
people asked `and how is Norman?´
and he was fine, always in good spirits.

An example to us all.

Until that Sunday when the struggle
grew too great and he relinquished
his strong hold on life and left us all to grieve.

All next day, in the cold bright sun,
people came and went, coming and going,
carrying condolences and funeral meats.

All day they came, to comfort the bereaved.

The coffin arrived in the afternoon
a cortege flanked by men;
relatives and friends, bringing Norman home.

And on the evening of the first day,
the house was filled with prayers
in every room, upstairs and down.

Folk dressed in black sat silently,
stood on the stairs. The minister prayed
the presenter sang the psalms.

And on the second day in the cold bright sun
people came and went and in the evening
once again the house was packed with folk in every room.

And on the third day, the funeral,
Again a day of cold bright sun. More people came
and more people came, crowd upon crowd.

Respectful men in dark suits, and black ties
stood outside. And inside, thoughtful women
sat close packed in every room.

The coffin lay in the porch, and close outside
the minister spoke words of comfort to the family,
praised the dead, reminded us how glorious he was in
life,

how memorable in death, and we sang psalms
divided into notes of mystery. And then the women
streamed into the light to join the men .

And six relations shouldered his coffin to the hearse
as mourners set off down the road to keep him company
along the way, to shepherd him towards his grave.

And deep into the ground he sank and those who would
scattered earth to cover him until his grave was filled
up to the brim and turves were ceremoniously trod.

We think of him, his life, his fun, his jokes, his struggle
day to day and our great loss and emptiness.
Norman, rest in peace.

TAKING IT FOR GRANTED

We wake under the same sky

I take a bath
fill my bowl
eat fresh bread
walk outside
smell wild flowers
hold my babies
kiss my man
dance in the rain
drink clean water
phone my friends
laugh out loud
say what I like
sing my song

Under the same sky you wake

silence is your song
outside is closed
fear chokes your empty bowl

EWES

You have to admire ewes
The way they give birth
to lambs year after year
without complaining.

The way they know how to mother,
even twins or triplets, fussing madly
in the first few weeks, feeding
on demand day and night,

baaing to bleating lambs
that have strayed too far away,
and standing firm against visitors
before scuttling off away from danger.

The way later on, to encourage
independence, if they're
not in the mood to suckle
they just sit down, or wander off

and the lambs have to make do
with just more grass. The way
they accept the inevitable day
when the lambs disappear

and after a few days baaing,
they just shut up. And it's strange how you
only notice how quiet they've been
when next years lambs are born.

And once the lambs have gone
you can't help admiring the way
they sashay down the road
in their black high hooves on gossipy outings.

Pregnant again, of course.

SPRING LAMBS

All day, lambs
obey their mothers
follow them, like sheep,
butting under to suckle
with vigorous wagging of tails.
All day they follow
as if the ewes expect it.

Then, just before sunset,
like children let out after tea,
they all run off together in a group
and race each other round the field
and leap up onto rocks
and spring into the air
startled, as if the earth's on fire.

It's a mad half hour
before bedtime.

SHEEP

'And we like sheep.....'
so the Hallelujah Chorus says.

It doesn't mean we like sheep.
A comma should come after 'we'

It means we are like sheep
and follow our leader where ever he goes.

Not all people do that.
And neither do sheep.

A flock of sheep is easily led, but one sheep
on her own has a mind of her own.

The word 'determined' is certainly
in her vocabulary and you could add 'stubborn'

A sheep that wants to get out, will get out,
and a sheep that wants to get in, will get in.

And when the grass is greener, which it is
on our side of the fence, she will get in.

Which is why we disagree in principle
with the Hallelujah Chorus.

ON THOSE DAYS

On those days
when we wake
to the sun
edging in

when we wake
to the silence
of no wind

when we amble
half moon beaches
apples in our pockets

when we sit small
on headland rocks
watching the sea

on those days
if this is all there is
it is enough.